# Ikeogu Oke

## *In the Wings of Waiting*

Ikeogu Oke is the author of three previous books of poetry, *Where I Was Born*, *Salutes Without Guns* and *Song of Success and Other Poems for Children*. Since 1988 his poems have appeared in print on both sides of the Atlantic in a variety of journals, including *Unity Magazine*, *Discovery* (published in Braille), *Farafina*, and *Prosopisia*, and in such webzines as *Ayaka* and *Saraba*. He has also performed his poems extensively at home and overseas. A native of Akanu Ohafia, in south-eastern Nigeria, he holds a BA in English and Literary Studies from the University of Calabar and an MA in Literature from the University of Nigeria, Nsukka. He has had an eventful working career, beginning as a maintenance crewman in the then National Electric Power Authority (NEPA). He has also been a consultant with several United Nations agencies and the Deputy Director of Communications and a Writing Instructor at the American University of Nigeria, Yola. He was a Standards Editor at Timbuktu Media Limited, Lagos (publishers of NEXT newspaper), and a media and communications aide to a Nigerian Minister of Power. He is currently the Media Adviser to the Chairman, Presidential Task Force on Power (PTFP), Abuja. In 2010, his second book of poems, *Salutes Without Guns*, was long-listed for the prestigious Wole Soyinka Prize for Literature and selected as one of the Books of the Year by the *Times Literary Supplement* (*TLS*).

**By the same author**

Poetry

*Where I Was Born*
*Salutes Without Guns*
*Song of Success and Other Poems for Children*

First published in 2012 by
Manila Publishers Company
21, Matadi Street, Wuse Zone 3
P. O. Box 10979, Area 10
Abuja 900001, Nigeria
Phone: +234-(0)803-453-1501
+234-(0)705-556-4595
+234-(0)808-234-8088
+234-(0)9-876-7171
Email: info@manilapublishers.com,
manila.publishers@gmail.com
Website: www.manilapublishers.com

ISBN 978-978-923-420-2

To Donna L. Miesbach, for faith

and

Amos N. Kalu, for kindness

# Acknowledgements

"A Little While" was first published in *All Things Will Die*, an anthology of poems in memory of Peter Areh, a Nigerian banker turned gallery owner and art connoisseur, murdered in Lagos on July 2, 2009. "My Country at Night" premiered (as a stage performance) at the Presidential Retreat for Power Sector Reform Investors held at the State House, Abuja, on October 14 and 15, 2010, and was first published in *Ayaka*, a webzine, as were "A Gandhian Prayer," "Yet You Walk with Them," "Portrait of a Praying Mantis," "To Wole Soyinka at Seventy-six," "A Precept Proven," "The Phantom," "Beach Scenery" and "Daughter." "Hard Words" (as "My Words Have Hurt You") and "Song of Adoration" were first published in *Prosopisia* (Vol. IV, No. 2, 2011), "An International Journal of Poetry & Creative Writing" published in India by the Academy of *raite(s)\** And World Literati (A.R.A.W.LII...). "Where Do We Go From Here?" was commissioned as a jingle for a campaign for Climate Change Adaptation by the Climate Change Adaptation Initiative sponsored by the University of Nigeria, Nsukka, and the African Technology Policy Studies (ATPS) and Open Society Foundations. "A Gandhian Prayer" was triggered by the unsuccessful attempt of the Nigerian writer Onyeka Nwelue to claim his prize monies in a literary competition from the organisers of the competition, one year after they announced him a double winner in the competition and in spite of his having widely publicised his grievance over the withheld earnings. "The Pledge," "I Can't Reach You," and "Maple Country" were first published in the special Music Edition of *Saraba* magazine for October-December 2011. My sincere thanks to all those behind these events—excluding those who withheld the writer's prize monies—and others from whom this work has received various forms of support, and especially to Okaa Christian Akamnonu, Dere Awosika, Bekinbo Dagogo-Jack, Clement Oke, Chuks Iloegbunam, Chike Madueke and Salisu Mohammed, for lasting surprises of moral and material goodwill.

I. O.

# Contents

## In the Wings of Waiting

# Foreword

## *In the Wings of Waiting*

Ikeogu Oke is not afraid to ask hard questions in the penetrating language only poetry has at its command. In our contemporary world where every day "A bomb blasts our sanity away" he also can use erotic language to express the other passion: for his country; and to give an equally passionate reproach in a turnabout stanza with the nation's failures:

> "Do you kiss me
> Because ... our teachers who yet await
> ...their monthly wages
> In the afterlife, as though they were
> The wages of sin...
> Or our doctors doomed
> To save lives
> With worse than bare hands?"

And in an erotic prose poem he reveals *the*: "Fathomless love of an ancestral home in a world of conflict that makes all, in a sense, homeless."

There is a state of Being in a song of love for women, country, other humans unknown to us in an individual existence:

> "A little while and we are gone
> Like trails of smoke when loaded guns
> Discharge their hoard."

The image coming with, from, a world surrounded by violence.

Omni-verse. The title of one of the sections into which he sees his work *pertaining* in deepest senses:

> "Is Africa sick...
> Is [it] dying because its meals
> Have long been spiced
> With the toxin...
> Of exploitation...
> ... with maladies [all] contrived?"

He has the poet's power to present in two lines the past-in-the-present:

> [...] "How often in the world's schemes of freedom
> And bondage have invisible chains replaced the visible."

And here's the third line set upon immediate time and place:

> [...] "the children of the Desert Spring [...]
> ...forever chase the chimera of freedom
> Down the shifting desert sand of their birthplace."

No end to the wide illumination in the protean gifts of this man. With a quote from Rabindranath Tagore: "Music is the purest form of art ... therefore true poets, they who are seers, seek to express the universe in terms of music"—suddenly you, the reader, discover summarily announced by Oke as "Appendix," the music scores which Ikeogu Oke himself has composed[1] and set some of his poems.

I cannot read, play music, hum to myself, so shall have to await the occasion when a friend can introduce me to this mode of Oke's splendid creativity. In whatever form of art, the poems *In the Wings of Waiting* are here for our personal and political association when our own words are not, as we survive, along with his insights, "the road to perdition."

— Nadine Gordimer

---

[1] The music was transcribed and arranged by Jude Nwankwo, my friend and associate, toward the production of the music scores, while I composed the melody. — The Author

# Preface

Poetry collections are usually an assortment of related or disparate compositions. But I have divided the poems in this collection into four segments, three of which are marked by a close sense of thematic affinity among the composite poems. In effect, the poems are largely related by themes such as patriotism, love, etc, and have been grouped together to convey the sense of such a relationship.

There is For Love of Country, a segment comprised of poems in various postures of celebratory, hortative and critical patriotism. There is Omni-verse, a sort of receptacle for an open-ended variety of poems, and the only unthemed segment. There is Paeans and the Self, a segment comprised of laudatory poems studded with hints of the autobiographical, some of which also provide a background for reflections on deeper (or broader) subjects, such as the following apostrophic lines from "To Wole Soyinka at Seventy-six":

> How I forgot that time
> Not only moves by flying;
> Even now it is marching forward,
> Inexorably, its feet in sturdy boots,
> Seeming to leave our dear land behind!

The eponymous segment, titled In the Wings of Waiting, is a sequence of fifty-two love poems, or, more precisely, fifty-two poems of love and desolation, as I have subtitled the segment.

The poems are to me proof that, for all its notoriety as a source of disappointment, falling in love remains one of man's most intriguing preoccupations. They add an emotive dimension to what, apropos of poetry, George Santayana described as "this intellectual and utilitarian language," and are examples of poetry as the product of the spontaneous articulation of powerful feelings in the heat and flux of experience, before tranquillity. For instance:

> I see you emerge from the shower;
> Your body is smooth like an apple;
> Your smile is the colour of apple juice;
> I bask like an agama in the fragrant warmth
> Of your exhalations, the perfumes your body breathes out;
> The electric rays bounce off your skin;
> The bells of your bosom ring me to silent awe.
>
> My body throbs; my loins twitch;
> My joy cannon stiffens, and rears
> To explode with seeds of children.

And:

> Woman of the East,
> Womb and cradle of light,
> I see you and a feeling strikes me
> As if the sun is rising from my heart,
> As if my heart will burst open
> With a million golden rays,
> A gazillion spindles of sharp, luminous joy.

Then (for a hint of the transition from love to desolation):

> Love, treasure slipping through my grasping hands,
> I had written you on scrolls of gold,
> Now I write you on parchments of lead
> From a heart whose pains
> Are achingly alive!

Some of these poems reinforce my commitment to bridging the gap between lyricism and musicality in poetry, resulting in the creation of poems as art songs—a species of formal music actualised to the point of their being accompanied by music scores, as with the following verses from "The Pledge" (whose music scores follow underneath):

> I love you more than tongue can tell,
> With a love that'll keep you glad and well,
> That'll shield you from the storms of life,
> And make you, most of all, my wife.
>
> Yes, when the storms of life shall break,
> Through every tremor, every quake,
> When the grounds you know may crack and shake,
> I'll be a protector for your sake.

## From "The Pledge"

*Words and Melody by* **Ikeogu Oke**
*Transcribed by* **Jude Nwankwo**

By making poetry muscal[1] in this way, an involvement that attests to my belief in form as an important element of poetry, I engage in the pursuit of improved and definitive craftsmanship in poetry—improved and definitive because it aims to create something permanent out of something beautiful, while enlarging the possibility of appreciating the beauty of the original thing by doubling its mode of presentation—in this case by annexing musical presentation to literary presentation. For if, in respect of form, lyricism and rhythm are the defining features of poetic composition,

---

[1]This volume ends with an appendix of music scores of some of the poems.

musicality is their ultimate expression, the highest manifestation of their physical beauty.

Poetry is words used at their fullest potential. And I think, without a doubt, that the poet should be first and foremost an apostle of beauty as the manifestation of elegant and measured expression in words; that he is a good poet insofar as he is devoted to this form of apostleship and will be a successful poet to the extent that he recognises that his art will be marked for proficiency to the degree that he chooses to treat beauty as the supreme value while not regarding it as the only value (for in poetry values relate not so much by aggregation as by hierarchy). Put otherwise, that he must set up his art as a medium for the exaltation and propagation of beauty among other lesser values such as theme, content and message; for these other values, important though they are in according solemnity to his work, will remain mute unless beauty speaks through them, or they through beauty. In short, he must seek first the kingdom of beauty, bearing in mind that other things will not be added to him as a result; but that he must also seek the other (important) things—preferably in such ways that their discovery and infusion into his work would be (or seem) spontaneous, as if arising from "a moment's thought," to invoke the words of W. B. Yeats[1].

My interest in the musicality of poetry is also reflected in a poem such as "Maple Country," a praise song for Canada. And one expects the reader to wonder why I, a Nigerian poet, would write a song in praise of Canada, even before I have visited the country. Not only do I intend, through the poem, to project poetry as an ambassador of goodwill; it is also my way of identifying with Derek Walcott's assertion that "you can't be a poet and believe in the division of man"—a recognition (since the division of man is an undeniable fact) that a poet's work need not be a recast of *the world as it is*, to modify V. S. Naipaul's famous dictum[2], but must interrogate its imperfections to the end of stimulating continuous improvement until they may cease to exist; as if—through his work—the poet should set the highest mark of idealism at which man might

---

[1] In his poem, "Adam's Curse."
[2] In *A Bend in the River*, his novel which begins with the dictum (whose main clause I paraphrase above): "The world is what it is; men who are nothing, who allow themselves to become nothing, have no place in it."

continuously aim by his conduct and, while inevitably falling short of that mark, constantly improve his character and the world by striving to attain it.

I attempt to set such a mark, for instance, in the poem titled "A Patriot's Prayer," an adaptation of the 35th poem in Rabindranath Tagore's *Gitanjali*, which also shows that the "charity" I express in "Maple Country" begins at home. Thus:

> Where the mind never knows fear
> and the head is always held high;
> Where knowledge is free,
> like the gift of rain from the sky;
> Where dreams are mapped without boundaries
> and the river of success drains into an ocean of possibilities;
> Where nationhood is an unbroken chain of people
> united in goodwill;
> ...
> Where the striving towards perfection
> can know no abatement and no end;
> ...
> Where each strives for all and the commonwealth
> is ever burgeoning for your sake;—
> Into that heaven of virtue, my Father,
> let my country awake.

Poetry is a tripartite being. Form is its body, content its spirit, message its soul. Neither the spirit nor the soul can become manifest except through the body. The body can be deformed for lack of skill by the poet, as a word architect, leaving the spirit and the soul with an ill-suited habitation in which their self-expression may become impaired. The spirit cannot be nobler than the poet's values. Nor can the soul be greater than his power to impress those values on others.

A perfect poem, which is invariably a great poem, is that which has succeeded in freezing the fleeting in the present, the eternal in the now, making the temporary irrevocably permanent. In any such poem the three elements I mentioned above as constituting the tripartite beingness of poetry blend without blemish, as in the 35th poem in Rabindranath Tagore's *Gitanjali*; as in the sonnet, "O World, Thou Choosest Not the Better Part," by George Santayana; as in Thomas Gray's "Ode on the Death of a Favourite Cat..."; as in

Robert Burns's "To a Mouse"; as in Robert Frost's "The Road Not Taken"; as in Seamus Heaney's "Scaffolding"; as in J. P. Clark-Bekederemo's "Streamside Exchange"; and myriad other works by the world's poets.

I continue to strive to produce such poetry, in which all the three elements are impeccably fused, while trying to paint my works on a universal canvas with as much bias to my natural origins as may be necessary to reinforce that intent without giving in to the lure of provincialism and the compromised sense of relevance it can engender; and I hope the reader will see this volume as a heart-felt, if perforce flawed, effort in that struggle.

Ikeogu Oke
Abuja
June 2012

# For Love of Country

"Patriotism is a form of piety. It is right to prefer our own country to all others because we are children and citizens before we can be travellers or philosophers."

— George Santayana

# A Patriot's Prayer

*This poem is an adaptation of the 35<sup>th</sup> poem*
*in Rabindranath Tagore's* Gitanjali

Where the mind never knows fear
    and the head is always held high;
Where knowledge is free,
    like the gift of rain from the sky;
Where dreams are mapped without boundaries
and the river of success drains into an ocean of possibilities;
Where nationhood is an unbroken chain of people
    united in goodwill;
Where the wind of truth is always pure
    and never still;
Where the striving towards perfection
    can know no abatement and no end;
Where the stream of reason flows unrestrained
    by any dam or any bend;
Where the dawn of each life breaks with ardent joy
and the dusk of each being glows without infirmity;
Where each strives for all and the commonwealth
    is ever burgeoning for your sake;—
Into that heaven of virtue, my Father,
    let my country awake.

# A Land of Rare Firsts

It was not the first time the bombs had gone off in our country in peacetime; but it was the first on an Independence Day, and thus we became the first nation to mark its jubilee with bomb blasts, murdering scores of its own in cold blood. What a distinguished nation!

It was not the first time the bombs had rocked our land in peacetime; but it was the first on the last day of December, and thus we became the first nation to ring out an old year and ring in a new with the bell of explosives, wasting scores of its own in cold blood. Yes, what a distinguished nation! A nation of two firsts in three months!

Our airplanes once nosedived, killing hundreds with the onset of elections. Now bombs are exploding like popcorn across the land as heralds of another election in a land that may well be the first to succeed in righting its past by wronging its future. A land of rare firsts!

Once parcelled with a letter, the bomb laid prone a prized journalist: Disembowelled, mangled, pulverised, bleeding and lifeless. And for once since Napoleon[1] the sword proved mightier than the pen; and it's our nation of rare firsts that made that possible!

Mightier because thirty years thence—or almost—the author of that letter has yet to be found; nor has the dispatcher, if not also the author; and for that long we have endured with queasy calm the braggadocio of that felony. And now new bombs have gone off at our national square and in market places—and in mosques and churches?—each more lethal than the last.

A bomb a day
Blasts our sanity away!

---

[1]Napoleon Bonaparte (1769-1821): a French military and political leader attributed with saying "the pen is mightier than the sword."

# Why Do You Kiss Me?

O that I have felt
The moist lips of this day
On my forehead—lips pressed
On my forehead in a kiss
Of congratulation—
The lips of my country,
My nation,
My fatherland—
Lips just turned fifty
In the service of growing old,
Of stacking up years for their own sake,
Lips that might have belonged to Judas.

Why do you kiss me,
Vain, unreflective land?

Do you kiss me
For our past
Was not happier
Than our present,
Though our present
Is richer than our past,
Richer as diamond than charcoal?

Do you kiss me
Because of our healthy hospitals
Or literate schools?
Or our teachers who yet await
Years of their monthly wages
In the afterlife, as though they were
The wages of sin?
Or our doctors doomed
To save lives
With worse than bare hands?

3

Tell me, why do you kiss me?
And with lips wrinkled with incompetence!

Do you kiss me to celebrate
Your profligacy, and flaunt
The new walls to the bastion
Of your impunity?

Do you kiss me to show off our roads
Filled with death gullies?
Do you kiss me to call attention
To the deadly shadows of our unelectrified nights,
As young and hooded hoodlums rule the land?

Why do you kiss me, even as wild besotted crimes
Run amok and cackle through the land?
Even as our factories have stopped working,
Why do you kiss me?

# Dialogue of the Spirit Beings

*Nine Nigerian Youths Debate Their Death*

A fortnight after they'd been laid to rest,
The Bauchi Nine[1] were gathered in a glade;
Now spirits, they were summoned by their mate,
To share thoughts that might mitigate their grief,
And thus reduce the sorrow that might plague
Their good souls in the world beyond the grave.
It was Kehinde[2] that summoned them
To that clearing ringed with giant trees,
Where they sat on tree stumps, each and all,
That formed a half-moon shape, a lunar curve.
It was a meeting primed for catharsis,
At which they held forth on our fatherland,
And, using words, explored their tragic fate;
Read below the very words they spoke.

**Kehinde:** Proud servants of our fatherland, what was our crime
That we were sent to our graves before our time?

**Seun:** Before our time? Don't you agree
That our death was due to destiny[3]?

**Eliot:** Destiny? Could destiny have ground a machete on a whetstone
To cut me off from life—and to the bone?

---

[1]The Bauchi Nine: an allusion to the nine Nigerian youths killed in Bauchi State, North Central Nigeria, in the 2011 post-election violence.
[2]Kehinde Jehleel Adeniji, one of the slain youths (see the preceding footnote); the others (in the order of their introduction in the poem) are: Seun Paul Adewunmi, Elliot Adowei, Ibrahim Sule Akonyi, Ebenezer Ayotunde Gbenjo, Ikechukwu Chibuzor Ukeoma, Anslem Chukwunonyerem Nkwazema, Tosin Olawale Teidi, and Obinna Michael Okpokiri.
[3]...Don't you agree/That ...destiny?: an allusion to a Nigerian politician's attribution of the death of the nine youths to "destiny."

**Ibrahim:** And those dagger thrusts that killed me
　　　　Were stabbings by the hand of destiny?

**Ebenezer:** And the spiked bludgeon that smashed my head
　　　　Was used by destiny in my killer's stead?

**Ikechukwu:** Alive, I was doused with petrol, and set alight.
　　　　And that, too, was a deed of destiny. Right?

**Anslem:** Hurray to destiny! Ally even of meticulous murder,
　　　　That slit my throat without the slightest bother?

**Tosin:** And shot me in the chest with a Dane gun
　　　　Under the hot glare of the Bauchi sun?

**Obinna:** That shot a poisoned arrow through my back
　　　　Even as I fled, pleading, in the dark?

**Kehinde:** But how would destiny strike, if it strikes,
　　　　With or without the bludgeon and its spikes,
　　　　Or any of the other weapons, as said,
　　　　That dispatched us to the land of the dead?

**Elliot:** It'd strike like what men would blame
　　　　When they'd rather set their name
　　　　Apart from their heinous deeds,
　　　　Or not reap the fruits of the vile seeds
　　　　They've sown—as of the grim crimes
　　　　That joined us with the dead before our times.
　　　　Indeed, it'd strike like the scapegoat of those
　　　　Who sought to bring us death without repose!

**Kehinde:** Is it then the case that destiny,
　　　　Blamed for the death of you and me,
　　　　Could not have used those hands
　　　　To manifest its grim designs for us?

**Seun:** Destiny's designs, to me, are like God's,
And mortals are the means their architect
Has often used to bring his will to be;
Nature is the other instrument,
Which bestows fortune as its opposite.
Thus, Judas was a hapless mortal tool
By which God's will was made to come to pass;
God's will as the serial prophesies
That Jesus Christ would die the way he did.
Can't we see that those prophetic words
Made the death of Jesus Christ destined;
And so his sad fate, being an end foretold,
Could be deemed as due to destiny?

**Kehinde:** Perhaps our blood was destined to be shed
For civil rule to take root in our land,
And Judas was not right to take his life,
Being destined to do the wrong he did?
By civil rule I mean the people's rule
Earned by voting when their ballot counts,
And winners are but proxies for the people,
Who serve to bring their sovereign will to pass.

**Elliot:** Judas was not wrong to take his life,
As proof that even destiny's proxies
Should pay for their vile deeds
Such as his—leading to another's death.
That Pontius Pilate and the baying mob
Still suffer odium for the death of Christ,
Though the death, as said, was prophesied,
Making it a death by destiny,
Also proves their lack of innocence
Who lend themselves to bring such death to be;
And such is the odium that, in Pilate's case,
Every thought of him evokes disgrace,
As though man's moral instincts must recoil
From his weakling's sly complicity,
As from Judas' greed and perfidy.

**Ibrahim:** Vile deeds are not pure for being
Due to destiny; they merely lengthen
The concatenation of evil and retribution
From whoever brings them to pass.

**Kehinde:** And if they don't?

**Obinna:** Evil men might blame their vile deeds
On mute destiny, and lay the wrong
Blame at its silent door,
Scorning morality, law and conscience!

**Kehinde:** What then should be their fate
Who snuffed out our lives
In a land ruled by law,
Conscience and morality?

**Tosin:** Whereas the law must stand to defend
Society's conscience and morality?

**Kehinde:** Yes.

**Ebenezer:** The law must prove itself
Not to be a lame leopard:
Unable to scare those
Who disturb its sleep.

**Anslem:** It must rise to defend all
For the good of all—and society—
And if or not our fate was what it was.

**Kehinde:** And ours is no disguised thirst for vengeance,
Due to regret for the lives we've lost?

**Ikechukwu:** To have died in the good service
Of one's fatherland
Is to have died nobly,
And no regret should
Attend such a death.

Or may I not like Horace just declare:
"It is sweet and glorious to die for one's country"?

At the end of these words
A single shroud of silence
Wrapped the nine,
As night fell over the glade
With a drizzle of starlight,
And each, nodding assent,
Arose to return straight
To whence he'd come.

# My Country at Night[1]

"Just as we have it in our power to banish
life-darkness; so are we the determiners of
light. And what light we can create."

— Michel Vickers

The stretch of darkness
Without the terror of ghosts
Bespeaks an elusive modernity.

"Civilisation not here," croak
Insomniac frogs in brackish gutters
Chocked with grime,
And deserted by moonlight—and starlight.
Must nature grace
Our folly
With such joys?

Darkness sits on our throne on high
In this nadir of nations
That has traded a long boom
For pitchy gloom,
And exiled light from its borders;
That has turned electricity
To a mere word
In the lexicon.

And fear, the sibling of darkness,
Reigns besides darkness;
Even now he prowls the lightless streets
On padded soles, masked, totting a gun,
Sneaking past the walls
Of silent factories,

---

[1]For the occasion of the Presidential Retreat for Power Sector Reform Investors held at
the State House, Abuja, on October 14 and 15, 2010.

Headed for the source
Of the next ransom,
In a land kidnapped
By darkness
And by fear.

Yet we're gathered here[1] for light,
For electricity,
For power,
For a new dawn whose night
Is not lit by stars and the moon alone,
Nor by smoky lanterns and candlelight,
As though in a land of endless beginnings,
A doomed, primeval land.

Yes, we're gathered here for light,
The light of faith and the light of work
That this land may yet rise from the nadir
To the crown of nations.

For how without bounds
We have found the cost of darkness!

---

[1] ...we're gathered here...: an allusion to the venue of the event at which the poem premiered (see the preceding footnote).

11

# A People's Dilemma

Trapped by a hideous ogre,
To be devoured one by one
Is the fate we must endure
In this womb of stone.

Even Odysseus, wiser
Than a tortoise
And craftier than a snake,
Would have been numbed by this:

Fiery snot oozing from the nose
Of our captor
Sprawled across this cavern's mouth
In full repose.

Is to chew bones like waffles
A feat that titillates or baffles?
He swallows flesh in lumps, roars with laughter,
And washes it down with blood—"Like water!"

But how long must we wait
To be preyed upon like this,
And please
Our self-appointed nemesis?

# Inquiries

*For Okey Ndibe*[1]

So you too are a threat,
Like honour, truth and justice
Have been to the lords
Of this land of ours,
And courage, and all the other virtues
Which the heavens hold dear?

So have they tried to stick
A hairpin in your tongue
As they did Cicero?

Have they tried to foist
A cup of hemlock on you
As they did Socrates?

What could be happening to you
At this dark harmattan hour
Whose cold bites with razored teeth?

Are you stripped and left alone
In a damp, dingy cell, your hands
Cupped over your twitching groin
As *their* shadows approach with long knives?

But you know the score,
And the gods have branded
You with courage stark and rare,
And fashioned you with a tongue
That must speak flames.

You cannot afford to be afraid;
Nor can we, your friends!

---

[1]A Nigerian writer and academic, following his detention by officers of the Nigerian State Security Service (SSS) on January 8, 2011.

13

# Yola

*A Love Pastoral*

Hot like live coal are the sands of the Sahara. But though my feet walk on them they will not feel hurt. I will cross the sands of the Sahara for your love. My feet will not feel their heat. Nor will they get burnt. Nor will I feel thirst for its waterlessness. Nor hunger while the quest for your love fills my being, and its goad drives me across the sands to an end I cannot fathom, across that endless waste of sand and heat.

Where the sand dunes are always rising, and the whirlwinds bridge the earth and sky, and the scorpion is proud of its fatal sting, the cobra of the deaths that dwell in its venom, and the spiders are gargantuan—as their faith in their lethal bite, and the camels are afraid of their footsteps—for what surprises may lurk beneath the sands? A sidewinder, perhaps, that has journeyed far from the Americas—to seek a higher stake in deadliness. Yet I will cross the same hot sands for your love's sake and will not feel a threat to my naked limbs or the soles of my bare feet.

Your feet will step on my pride and go home with the unfading fragrance of a loyal rose. For my love is such that will take all things, bear all things, endure all things—even the spit of your proud scorn and the taunts of your mock—even if not mock—rejections. But what shall it profit me to gain the whole world and lose your love?

Yola is still stretched in a rock basin sunk amid high hills whose backs turn green with the rains and brown with the harmattan. It is still the land of extreme heat and extreme cold, where the stout baobabs and rugged acacias rule the savannah that ever stretches farther than the eye can go, and big-horned cows graze tranquilly in the season of greenery, and mares suckle their young in eternal grasslands under the moon's proud watch. There the Benue still glides along on its peaceful course to meet the Niger that roars at their confluence of calm and turbulence.

14

The times have swept the grasslands bare of their lushness. They have ripped the baobabs bare of their leaves. Even the long-suffering acacias are leaf-nude and shivering from windblasts. And the haze of the harmattan hangs over the city of my good Lamido[1], hangs like an ancient cloud of fog. Not long ago, they were bright with the brightness of your Nubian cheer. Now they're no longer bright. Nor are they dark but bat-like for the weather they have sprung upon the city—neither fully land nor aerial lives. The winds howl in the distant skies but bear no auguries of rain. The breezes sweep the scorched grasslands but bear no solace of moisture. The Yola of my dreams has become a jewelled city scorched by the harmattan. Her minarets sizzle in the heat. The domes of her mosques are browned from its showers of dust. Yet beauty is not what we see that our eyes may bristle and gape with wonder, like your beauty—proud woman of the savannah!

It is no light prey to the elements. And nasty weathers cannot touch its soul, its essence. It is like love, true beauty, eternal, the all-weather love of life for our flawed earth. Its passion burns slowly and does not die: the quiet glow of moonlight, the cool radiance of the dawn, the gentle glare of the twilight, the fluorescence of the Phoenix so swanlike in its resurrection, sparkling white with soulful melodies, with songs that merge time with timelessness, as I long to merge my soul with yours.

Long had I stood behind the gridiron and dreamt of my tongue tickling your sweet navel, and of my thumb strumming your bosom like the strings of a mandolin, and of your silhouette of perfect beauty floating away beyond the banks of the Benue to the end of the green hills, and past where the gloaming drowns with its golden light in the aquamarine of the farthest grasslands, and then up to the skies whence the sun has just descended, and then turned white and invisible as it merged with the distant clouds.

And Yola was the bed of those dreams!

---

[1]Lamido: traditional ruler of the Adamawa people whose ancestral home is Yola in northeastern Nigeria; but the referent here (i.e. "my good Lamido") is Dr. Aliyu Musdafa (1922-2010), the Lamido of Adamawa when this poem was written.

You're a proud lioness. It's in your eyes. And how proud I'll be to sire your cubs, and bring home a constant kill of prey: deer and zebra, and little duikers when the times are lean, and range far afield to scour the Serengeti for your favourite of all prey—the wildebeest. And we shall have a one-wife pride littered with happy cubs!

Have you seen the ram that rules the northern grasslands? A gangly lord of many harems, his fur is white like milk, and mottled with a creamy blackness; and the winds carry his bleating far afield, far beyond the banks of the Benue; and he herds his wives from the shed by dawn, and their children to the shed by dusk; and he leads them to the green grazing places beside the still waters, and their voices bleat in unison: *Mmeeeee! Mmeeeeeeee! Mmeeeeeeeeeeee!* His scrotum tips on the low grass when he walks; and it is huge with the hugeness of his royal balls. A great father, he has raised many sheep for the Salah feast, and many more for the fragrant flames of the *mai suya 's*[1] grill. And many more shall he raise before the sunset sinks above his reign, and a younger buck usurps his throne, and drives him off, wifeless, childless, alone, to wonder desolate beyond the grasslands of his royal days. And then his wives' udders shall be for lambs sired by another male!

Have you seen the cows returning from pasture? A mere lad herds them; he wears a straw hat daubed with bright colours, and holds his goad aslant behind his back, and whistles a jaunty tune, and leads them from behind. At his finger even the wildest licks itself to submission, and will stay subdued unto death: everything bends at the kind wand of love, even these huge beasts of the Yola grasslands.

---

[1]*Mai suya*: a man who sells grilled meat called *suya* in Nigerian parlance.

16

# Paeans and the Self

# Maple Country[1]

*The Canada Day Song*

Land of the leaf like the open hand,
Vast, free-giving and warm,
Land of the red maple leaf,
We salute you!

**Chorus:** All hail! Beautiful land!
Glorious indeed and noble!
Let's drink a toast to Canada!
A worthy country!

It is your day and we have gathered,
Friends with hearts as warm as yours;
Joy is your victual we share,
Maple country!

Land of free tongues equally loved,
Free-giver of grace and good health;
O, land of peace and gentle strength,
We salute you!

It is your day and we are here,
Friends of the earth and friends for you,
To honour you and share your joy,
Maple country!

---

[1] Composed in response to my invitation by the Canadian High Commission, Abuja, to the 144th Canada Day Party held on Thursday, June 30, 2011, at the Sheraton Hotel, Abuja.

# Chinua Achebe

*An 80<sup>th</sup> Anniversary Tribute*

The great river of his life has fed many rivulets,
And earned for this unbounded gratitude;
Of our rivers he is the Nile,
Leisurely in its flow and steadfast,
Serving myriads on its timeless course.

Sage and raconteur,
His stories ride the backs
Of many lands
In their watery journeys
Round the world;
Chronicler when *Things Fall Apart*
And are *No Longer at Ease*
In the *Anthills of the Savannah*,
And of other wonders of our world.

Young leader of the charge of truth
While the minds of many heroes
Still slept in their scabbards;
The first pure ray
Of the light
Of our undimmed culture.

The great awakener
Of our continent from the hard couch
Of complacency;
The one who lit a lamp
In the darkness and cut a path
Through the thicket,
Showing the way
To our cultural pride and freedom
From where the rain
Started to beat us.

The dogged flower
That blooms
In grounds soft and hard,
Whose fragrance
Encircles the globe,
And whose sunny radiance
Lights souls with gratitude,
Dazzles brightly
Through another dawn!

# To Wole Soyinka at Seventy-six

When I heard the news,
That you have turned seventy-six,
I wished that time
Could shed its wings
And forever stop flying,
That your years
May stand still,
Frozen in virtue and stateliness,
And your age ageless,
That your good deeds
May not be bound to time.

How I forgot that time
Not only moves by flying;
Even now it is marching forward,
Inexorably, its feet in sturdy boots,
Seeming to leave our dear land behind!

# He Walked Upon This Land

## Or

## Song of a Legacy

*For Atiku Abubakar, on the occasion of the 2007 Founder's Day of
the American University of Nigeria, Yola*

O that he walked upon this land!

And we are massed upon this land,
Pilgrims with light and joyous hearts,
Massed upon this land with thanks for
He walked upon this land.

In the end we shall still be in need of words,
Though we were deluged with words
To give voice to our thanks that
He walked upon this land.

And the future, which was just yesterday
Though we shall ever expect it, shall fill
Our hearts with rejoicing for
He walked upon this land.

And the past, which ever goes by and yet
Never arrives, shall stir our minds
With fond recollections for
He walked upon this land.

In the days of Lamido Aliyu Musdafa
The Turaki Adamawa walked upon this land:
He left this glory of a school as
He walked upon this land.

This footprint which time shall only make more deep,
This ever-quickening breath of knowledge's air,

He left it as
He walked upon this land.

O that he walked upon this land!

And we are massed upon this land,
Pilgrims with light and joyous hearts,
Massed upon this land with thanks for
He walked upon this land.

# Yet You Walk with Them

*For BB*[1]

"A thing of beauty is a joy forever;
Its loveliness increases."

— John Keats

Legs that should be hanging
In the Louvre, hanging by
Golden chains in armoured glass casings,
Two perfect works of sculpted art
From hip joint to their toenails tipped
Each with a bright crescent meniscus...

Legs straight like arrows, the pride
Of Vulcan's foundry and his forge,
Or so they seem, with the metallic-golden
Tincture of a hue that hugs
Their radiant skins like supple foils...

Straight legs but for the cusps
Of soft knees and softer calves
Like ridges stretched behind
And heels high like the peak
Of Everest...

Legs that should, yes, be hanging
In the Louvre, above the plinths
Of the *Pietà*
And the *Nike of Samothrace*...

Yet you walk with them
And trample earth's low sod
With their careless soles,
Careless of what beauties they exude.

---

[1]BB: Beautiful Brains, my fond alias for the subject of this poem and the subsequent three.

# Body Music

*For BB*

Again I have looked!
And what do I see?

A symphony of straight lines
And perfect curves,
Eyes adazzle with hidden powers,
Lips bold with hints of sensuality,
Thick and smooth like an apple's orb,
And lusciously succulent.

O that the thought of them
Has made me a master brewer
With words, reeling in
Divine intoxication!

And I have seen
The tame tigress within,
Whose fearless heart still glances
Through your humane eyes.

And seen femineity:
Your sweet pulp
Of true womanhood
Beneath a hard exterior,
Like watermelon.

But how long must I
Paste my ears to the wind[1]
To catch the strains
Of your body music?

---

[1]Paste my ears to the wind: A similar expression occurs in line 4 of "Fear," a poem by the Nigerian poet Kalu Uka.

# The Escort of Twilight

*For BB*

The evening
Brought you out
Again, and led you
To the blue dais
Of my memory,
Your neck decked
With a necklace
Of white steel,
An imprimatur of style,
A cocky elegance.

And I would stand tongueless
And ponder those words
I could not say,
And those hands
I could only wish to take,
Delicate even to the touch of sight,
Emitting a sanitary fragrance.

Beauty poured down
From your presence
Like a cascade, a rumbling
Stream of water
From a precipice
Veiled with white spumes
And whiter vapours.

And the deep valley
Acclaimed the sight
With thunders of applause!

# The Phoenix

*For BB*

The grey and white and blue
Hues of heaven
For a backdrop,
Your picture stands
On my desktop.

The look in your eyes
Is oyster-soft, softer
Than a woman's eyes should be
When love drips beneath
Their watery veils.

The hair rolls down
To your shoulders
In driblets.
Your earrings are rhomboids,
The colour of wrought iron.
A silver pendant rests
On a silver chain in the deep
Groove of your bosom.
Your head is the shape
Of the perfect pear,
Down to a tapering jaw.

A dark suit!
A purple blouse!
Lips pink and unfurled
Like the petals of a rose!

Beautiful woman,
You have set
My imagination alight;
It is burning up
To rise from its ashes
And soar again.

# The Testimonies

*For a pretty woman, on her 51st birthday*

Tongues have called you beautiful;
Hearts have called you beautiful;
The testimonies of my eyes
And of my heart say
They do not flatter,
That they are tongues and hearts
Of truth spoken to the mind's acclaim
What the eyes can see and have seen.

Yours is the beauty of the full moon
When the night clouds
Are pitch black and her bright orb
Rolls along their backs with lucid beams,
Her warm cheer melting away
The gloom from their icy hearts...

And of a dogged skiff
That has ridden the storms of age
And beached on a fortunate isle
At the dawn of twilight,
Her golden light streaming through
Her grizzled hair of mast
And stern and prow.

But beauty only of the body
Is a sweet lie told by lucky genes.

For true beauty is a light
That shines from the soul,
Kindled by love for humanity—
And it's as great
As that love is deep—such beauty
As those tongues and hearts
Have said inhabits you!

# Impressions from a Reading

*For a woman who prefers anonymity*

Your nose stood out among the noses in the room,
Like an arrow with a slight bend to its shaft.
I have seen pointed noses: I have loved the broad sharpness
Of yours, but far more have I loved that bend
For which it stands out among its countless kind.

Then there was that glint, the glint on the tip of that nose,
Which stretched forth into my eyes
As it stood pulsing on your face.
Did you get to know of that glint?
And that your nose sometimes glowed?
Or was it just my optical illusion?

I did not see you stand, but you stood tall sitting down,
And I wondered how you would stand
If you were to be standing!

# Eight Years After

*For Dobleme Ettah*

That fire has not dimmed,
That flame
That glows
Behind your irises,
Beneath your closed eyelids,
Glows visibly,
That smouldering incandescence
Of cheer,
Of hope,
And perhaps love.

That smile
Still mounts
Your lips
Triumphant,
Rides upwards
To your forehead,
Waving a flag
Of defiance
Above a blistered heart.

That your body's
Catfish beauty remains,
Albeit more full,
More rounded,
Inviting awe!

# Daughter

Daughter of the open air
Daughter of skies never ending
Daughter of vistas without borders
Daughter whose oceans bridge earth and sky
Daughter of savannahs with neither edge nor boundary
Daughter of truth imperishable
Daughter of high ideals, higher than hills and clouds and
    heavenly places
Daughter of the fine heart of art and science
Daughter of silences echoing with love unspeakable
Daughter of the eternal seasons cyclic and evergreen
Daughter of the horseback of impossibilities
Daughter of the dauntless bark on the tip of crested waves
Daughter of geysers of possibilities, bursting through the skies
Daughter of the universe of deep roses and cheerful lilacs
Daughter of time still and yet in motion
Daughter of the brown earth and the blue cosmos
Daughter hard as diamond and soft as a lily
Daughter of endearing contrasts and alluring unities
Daughter of love whose name means dove
Daughter of beauty whose pivots are form and grace
Daughter of feathers dancing in a whirlwind
Daughter of desert fruit baskets, of oases ringed with the camel's
    pleasure
Daughter of ease and gravity
Daughter of this never-ending poem
Daughter, daughter, my daughter...

# In Three Years

In three years,
You have become
The salt of my life,
Out-flavouring the will to power.

In three years,
You have become
The joy of my life,
Out-sweetening the nectar of love.

In three years,
You have become
The light of my life,
Outshining the beam of truth.

In three years,
You have become
The spice of my life,
More aromatic than the thyme of passion.

In three years,
You have taught me
That love is responsibility,
And I am grateful, my child.

# A Little While

*For Peter Areh*

A little while and we are gone,
Like trails of smoke when loaded guns
Discharge their hoard,
Like the echoing sound when loaded guns
Discharge their hoard,
And ever the pendulum of our hearts
Ceases to swing, ceases to beat.

And they who load the guns
Shoot to death their fears and jealousies,
And that for which they fret at excellence:
Their blighted concourse with mediocrity,
That tyrant who enslaves with chains of spite.

Or do they truly shoot to death
Their fears and jealousies,
And that for which they're scared of excellence:
Their blighted union with mediocrity,
That despot who enslaves with chains of spite?

With you they shot at the spirit of a flying meteor,
An embodied soul quick like a shooting star,
Trailing the shimmering hues of the rainbow,
A radiant life decked in the seven colours
That merge in white light.

And should we say "forgive them"
Even if they knew what they did?

# Two Spaniards

Two Spaniards have come
Calling at our office,
Calling twice in as many days,
Settling in the same lowly seats
On both visits,
Like sediments of good cheer
In the warm glasses
Of our hospitality;
One named Irama Vega Pueyo,
The other Juan Carlos Jover,
They were a charming pair,
Like the Great Bear
Beside a blue crescent moon.

Bringers of good humour
And better wine,
Not theirs the frozen airs
That stifle genuine warmth
Among the races,
A prince of camaraderie
Beside his equal half,
Equal in her power
To strike with joy!

Time rose lightly
On the warm currents
Of their presence,
And soared away
On spread and silent wings,
Till night crept in on us unnoticed;
And yet the room glowed
With the presence
Of the two Spaniards!

# Omni-verse

# Is Africa Sick?

Is Africa sick
Because it should be sick?
Is it sick like a horse whose fodder
Is rigged with germs?
Like a bird whose wings
Are shot through with arrows?
Is it sick with a contrived sickness?

Is Africa dying
From the disease
Of old age?
Or from having
Put its neck
In the noose?
Is it dying
Because it should
Be dying or dying
A death contrived?

Is it dying because its meals
Have long been spiced
With the toxin of misrule,
Its drinks laced
With the poison
Of exploitation?

Is it sick and dying
Because it should be sick
And dying or sick and dying
With maladies all contrived?

# The Desert Spring

A blood-rimmed dawn breaks across
The desert dunes, the golden dunes
Of the vast Sahara; eddies of lacquered dust
Swell and rise and bridge the shifting desert ground
And the searing face of the moistureless sky.

A dust-to-dust dawn: at its light
Ten million voices rise in tumult, flailing
Like the storms of an angry sea, ten million voices
Billowing with ten million echoes call for freedom,
And the sound of their fury rises as if borne aloft
By the swift spirals of cold air and golden dust.

Not long ago, I glimpsed as in a dream two crypts
Like man-made mountains, abodes of long-rested kings,
Rise on boulder feet and with rocky arms lurch towards
The dawn—Oh, was it the dawn?—sinking in the West,
Right beside the cradle of daytime, and furious eyes
Burned with clenched teeth on their frontal slopes,
As they made to halt the twilight-dawn.

Ah! How often in the world's schemes of freedom
And bondage have invisible chains replaced the visible,
Unbeknown to those who wore the two! May theirs not
Be so replaced—the children of the Desert Spring—and may
They not forever chase the chimera of freedom
Down the shifting desert sand of their birthplace.

# Where Do We Go From Here?

Where do we go from here?
When our hot earth
Cracks to its core,
And dreadful-dark tsunamis charge at us?

Where do we go from here?
When the deserts
Eat up our farmlands,
And famine strips our barnyards to the bone?

Where do we go from here?
When rain falls
No more or in excess,
And droughts or floods become our only lot?

There's nowhere to go,
Nowhere!
And so let's nurse our planet
Back to health.

# The Phantom

He glittered when he walked into the room,
Wearing a chandeliered smile,
Her imaginary groom.
The thermopile
Of her heart lost its restraint
For a charm it could not contain
As he walked into the room,
Her imaginary groom.

A perfect gentleman richly clad
In the latest fad,
Was he going to be riches
Reduced to a skull[1]
With all the gory lessons it teaches,
A bony ball of nothing after all?

Her heart sings
Of his butterfly radiance
Flitting heavenwards on fluffy wings,
"It's ascent and grace in a charmed dalliance!"

Her heart sings, sinks, sings!

---

[1]Reduced to a skull: an allusion to the transformation of the "perfect gentleman" in
Amos Tutuola's *The Palm-wine Drinkard* to a skull.

# The Road to Perdition

*"Ụzọ dị nma a agaa ya nga abụọ."*

Trans: "If a road is good we travel it twice."

— An Igbo proverb

"Tell her," he said to the emissaries, "that she never knew how much I valued what she broke."

"Nobody can judge an internal injury," he had said, "by the size of the superficial wound, of the hole."

— Salman Rushdie[1]

She waits on a road
To which he should never return,
Where death, a cudgel in hand,
May stalk his every step from the shadows.

The gulf between them is now so deep
That time may sleep
In its bed
And wake up dead.

The sage in Rushdie
Once wrote of "the nature
Of the unforgivable."
And every angel in Hell
Is proof that even
The grace of God
Is not without bounds,
That His love to pardon
Has its limits too.

---

[1]Both quotes are from Salman Rushdie's anecdotal illustration of "the nature of the unforgivable" in *The Satanic Verses*. (See page 404 of the Viking Penguin edition of the book).

And how the bed of that gulf
Is laid with sins
That even God might not
Have thought possible,
Like those of a wife
Who killed the unborn child
Of her husband, and spilt
Its blood upon
Their nuptial bed!

Doesn't she see trails
Of that blood on the road
On which she now stands,
Beckoning him?

# Beach Scenery

Glowing, red-hot, the disc
Of the twilight lowers
Into the sea.

I listen for a hiss
And hear none,
A hiss as when
A blacksmith
Dips hot iron in water,
His bellows chockfull
With blazing coal.

And I think of the red-hot
Disc from nature's foundry
Of heat and silence,
The hot, hissless, seaward gloaming.

# Samsa II[1]

Or

Roommate

With its hard, chitinous armour,
The scotched roach lies face up
On the night's cold floor
And kicks its broken legs
In the night's cold air;
Its antennae twist, flail hysterically,
As it shudders in the throes of death,
And then lies still:
*Memento mori!*

---

[1]Samsa II: an allusion to Gregor Samsa, the character in Franz Kafka's "The Metamorphosis" who wakes up to find himself transformed into a monstrous insect.

# A Gandhian Prayer

*A song, to be chanted, preferably, with instrumental accompaniment, and with solemnity*

"... pray for them which despitefully use you."

— Matt 5:44 (AV)

Dear Lord, never cease to grant your favours
To those who prey on writers and their labours;
May their barns be ever filled with money,
May their days be ever bright and sunny,
May their children never cease to prosper
In health and riches, as is fair and proper;
And may their wives be happier than they wish,
And never let their blessings diminish.

And if they think it's human to be mean,
That it's their hapless victims they demean,
Dear Lord, raise their poor souls from the gutter
In which, like drunken elves, they crawl or totter,
Then cure their blindness that their eyes may see
That there's no virtue in dishonesty.

## Portrait of a Praying Mantis

He perches behind a shaft of tall grass
And prays for a prey to pass
From the shrubbery underclass.

Insect and insectivore,
He prays with fervour
For an unwary soul to devour,
Robed in a green cassock,
Hidden behind a green shaft of tall grass.

Hands piously clasped,
Working his mandibles with fervent words,
He asks his god:
"Would it be another wiggly worm,
A crawling ant,
Or perhaps a hopping grasshopper this time,
For he who must feed
On the wretched of the earth?[1]"

"Send something, Lord,
Send something,
For your servant
Tarries, hungry," he prays,
As he rubs his silent palms,
And wipes his anxious lips repeatedly.

Many a hapless prey
Have I seen him digest
Posed like a statue
In diligent prayer.
Many!

---

[1] "… the wretched of the earth" recalls the title of a book by Frantz Fanon.

# The New Colossus

A savage king bestrides an iron throne
And clobbers virtue with a whalebone
Grasped in his tight, calloused fist,
A band of cowries strapped about his wrist.

His feet are bound with leather thongs;
In his spare hand the three prongs
Of a trident flash an argent blaze,
Thrust in the path of the sun's rays.

Is he greater than he who paced the same
Palatial grounds with terror and came
To ruin suckling at a nymphet's poisoned breasts,
The goggled one who roared and barked behests

Across the land? Greater or not,
Time shall undo the grim knot
That's tied our fates together,
Helpless in a dream-corroding weather.

# In the Wings of Waiting

**(Fifty-two Poems of Love and Desolation)**

# I
# Impassioned and Passionate

Impassioned and passionate,
I search in vain for the words
To say how much I love you,
How much I would love to care.

The words grope in the dark cavity
Of my mouth and cannot find their way out;
They are trapped forever in a buccal cave,
Lost even to their own minds and memories.

Vain and desperate words, doomed never
To find birth in the world of men.
What would they say if they were born?
Like what would they look?

Nothing! The dregs of pallor!
Yes, they would say nothing
And look like the dregs of pallor—those blank
And feeble words!

For what can they say about that
Which even the Muses cannot convey,
A love lost to the minds of divinities,
The thought of whose depth
Must freeze even the vocal cords
Of those maidens who reign
In the heavenly realm of words,
The nine daughters of Zeus?

Sweet Muses, do not desert me for your incapacity.
O! That I can only hear the rumblings of your silence
And can even now see your sleek tongues
Glued to the edge of your awed palates,
Yet do not desert me as I try.

## II
## Just for Your Sake

Awake before dawn,
Thoughts of you flood my mind,
Of your tangerine beauty,
Your bright armour of good looks,
Then hints of your enduring goodness,
Your beauty stashed within,
A hoard of hidden treasures,
And that you will love me
In the fullness of time
Much as I love you,
And we shall build a nest together,
Of twigs of resilient hope,
Of faith that time cannot erode,
And hatch our love eggs
And raise our hatchlings together,
You and I, eternal lovebirds,
Living happy.

And we shall plant
In the morning
And reap
In the evening.

And we shall sow
With the sunrise
And reap
With the gloaming.

And we shall plant
By dawn
And reap
By the trail of sunset.

And the old age of our love
Shall be golden, and pour

With radiant showers
Down the sky.

And the juice of ageing
Shall taste like the sherbet of youth,
Sweet and piquant,
Just for your sake!

And our love shall be reckoned
Like the life of the stars,
With a beginning and an end
Only to be imagined,
And be timeless like the seas
And ageless like the mountains,
And be assured
Like the coming of the seasons,
Etched in deep concentric cycles,
And the rainbow shall foretell its future
With bright prophetic hues.

## III
## Dark with a Nubian Shadow

Your lips are dark
With a Nubian shadow;
They are sweet to the look
And visible
Even when you are not here.
Your eyes are like the dawn
Sliding skywards
On the slopes
Of the Kilimanjaro;
They are bright
With a Nubian lustre,
And half-seen when you're away.
Even the sheets are stained
With the incense of your absence,
Fragrant remembrances
That burn your memories
Into the mind
Like a birth mark
As the morning yearns for you
From where the night left off,
And the noon
Burns to quench the thirst
Of my longing
For your smile.

## IV
# A Moth at the Globed Light

A moth at the globed light
Of your love, I flap my wings
In throbbing ecstasy, and shed
The wing-dust of my joy
On the ground before your feet.
I savour the pleasure
Of waiting for you
And my moth-belly
Rocks with protuberance,
A host to light pendulums of delight.

When again shall I see that squint
In your eyes when you laugh?
When again shall I
Behold your cackle?
For yes your cackle
Is visible: rainbows of confetti
Tumble out of your mouth
When you laugh loud,
Your ribs shuddering
To pump them out
Through your parted lips,
In gentle sprinklings.

## V
# I Can't Reach You[1]

I can't reach you!
What am I to do?
I feel my breath is cut off;
O yes I'm in love.

Please call me once you can;
I want to be your man:
To love you like no other,
More truly than a mother.

**Chorus**[2]: Baby, baby, I'm waiting,
Baby, baby, I'm waiting,
I want to be your man,
Please call me once you can.

Baby, baby, I'm waiting,
Baby, baby, I'm waiting,
To love you like no other,
More truly than a mother.

I'm waiting by the phone;
I wait for you alone;
I wait and gasp to hear
Your voice from far or near.

Please call me, baby, call me;
Please don't leave me at sea;
I'll wait from dawn till nightfall;
I'm waiting for your call.

---

[1] A pop art song.
[2] To be sung after the first two and last two stanzas.

58

## VI
## A Lozenge of Flesh

You are lusciously
And tantalizingly made!

I want to give you a tongue bathe;
I want to lick you up
Like a lozenge of flesh,
I'll always be right there by your side
And give you every support you ever needed.
Your vision will be my mission,
Your glance my admonition.
When your eyes speak I will hear;
When your heart calls I will listen;
When your thoughts beckon I will come;
When your mind summons I will obey;
For a true woman is a creature
Of unerring instincts;
And you are a true woman,
One to guide me
With the compass
Of an unfaltering soul
As I navigate
The doubts of life's seas!

And you will lead me
To berth on happy isles
And beach on fortunate shores
Where the sights of pearls
From oysters *who* transform life's irritations
To rare gems await me—an aqueous paradise!

And you will lead me by the leash
Of my love that still confounds
The best daughters of Olympus,
That has frozen their tongues
And turned their gem-like words
To gritty ashes, though they speak through me.

And you will lead me to that blazing throne
Where truth, honour, justice, and all the rest
Of the best ideals bow down to love,
The Throne of the Paradise of Virtue!

And I, trusting in your infallible instincts,
Will follow till the end of my days.

# VII
## Beauty and Transcendence

Your looks have fused beauty
And transcendence
The way the passing of time
Fuses the ascent of the dawn
With the luminescence of daylight
And the descent of twilight
With the shadowiness of nightfall;
The joints are imperceptible
Like the seams of a continuum.

You are to me like sunlight
Among the Eskimos:
Warm, radiant and rare,
A blessing I could never wish to part with.
And how could I bear the thought
Of your absence, of a full life
Without the warmth
Of your presence,
Marooned as I must be
Among the icicles?

How could I, smitten by the conscience
Of your love, ever think
Of life without your love,
Of my back towards that radiance
Which has lent a permanent glow
To my gloomy heart,
A gentle flush of cool light till now unknown?
Even now the gentle fireworks
Crackle on my lips
In an unconscious smile
At the thought of your sweet ways;
They crackle and glint,
And their colour is a golden purple.

## VIII
## Your Name among the Stars

I want to make you immortal;
I want to enshrine your name
Among the stars; I want at the end
Of our days to leave in the night-heavens
A constellation emblazoned with your name,
So your days will know no end;
And all the denizens of all the worlds
Shall look up at the night-sky
And behold the letters of your name
Stretched across an invisible banner
Over the face of your constellation.

O that the frozen tongues
Of the Muses may come loose
And let me, thawed by the warmth
Of my love for them, set free
By the warmth of my love for you!

O that they may come loose
And let me. And what can hold
The tongues of the nine maidens,
Daughters of the ruler of the gods?
What can hold their tongues ice-bound
But a love so deep and incomprehensible,
This love of a moth for the light
Of its soul's preservation?

## IX
## My Tummy Rocks with Pleasure

My tummy rocks with pleasure:
Your cherubic face floats
Across my sight, and yet
My eyes are closed;
A round face, berry-sweet
And smooth like an apple
Polished to bounce off
The rays of moonlight.

*Opuriche n'abali*[1],
May I pick your absent nose
With my tongue? O, how
You make my pleasures
Come easy and affordable
Even now that you are away!

I shall celebrate you,
I shall sing your praise,
For you treat me as a lioness
Treats her lion and her cubs,
And my weakness is not your strength.

The lioness: she is the wisest
And noblest of the female beasts
Of the wild, the model of wifely submission.
For, yes, there also are beasts
Of homes and royal houses,
Domestic and palace beasts,
Men and women who prey
On their fellows worse than wild beasts.
The lioness: loyal wife, devoted mother,
Diligent provider for her lion and cubs,

---

[1]*Opuriche n'abali* (Igbo): The special one of night-time.

63

And their weakness is not her strength.
My tame lioness, I wish you are
Here with me, where
My weakness is not your strength,
As it is not anywhere else.

# X
# Like Yesterday

It's one of those days,
When your face
Out-glows the dawn,
And your smile
Is a clear river
Flanked by rainbow banks,
And your soul loves
To lie naked
On the noontide beach,
Assured of her spotless beauty,
And your looks are warm,
And soft, with a wistful
Haze of solitude,
And your mind,
A wingless angel, buoyant and pure,
Floats leisurely over
The tides of time,
Like yesterday!

# XI
## Heart of Golden Hearts

As is a heart so are its affections.

Yours is not a kiwi heart
That cannot take off the ground;
It is an eagle heart whose realm
Is the wide expanse of the blue sky.
It is the heart of a rare lioness
Resolute in her pursuit of the prey
Of absolute values, not to kill but to preserve.
It is the heart of a gazelle
Beautiful in its mystic leaps of ecstasy.
It is a heart fashioned
At the forge of divine truth,
Hammered to perfection
At the anvil of the gods,
Whose tincture bears shades
Of strength, honour, compassion,
And all the other finer virtues.
It is the heart of golden hearts.

## XII
# From the Shower

I see you emerge from the shower;
Your body is smooth like an apple;
Your smile is the colour of apple juice;
I bask like an agama in the fragrant warmth
Of your exhalations, the perfumes your body breathes out;
The electric rays bounce off your skin;
The bells of your bosom ring me to silent awe.

My body throbs; my loins twitch;
My joy cannon stiffens, and rears
To explode with seeds of children.

How can I not be grateful for my luck?
I do not deserve you;
I cannot possess you;
I can only seek to adore you,
And be the high priest of your rare charm,
Your exquisite goodness,
And seek by the power of my Muse
To make you a peer of the stars on high.

# XIII
## Your Father Says No

Now your father says no
I know I have just reached
The first of the seven mountains
I can climb and the first
Of the seven seas I can swim across
To earn your love, fourteen obstacles
Yet unknown to fact or legend.

For what is love if it comes
With such ease with which the dawn
Climbs the invisible mountain
Of the sky to reach the equinox,
Wearing to its peak a rosy smile,
Or with which the brooks of my birthplace
Have traced forever their watery course,
Gurgling ever from their fountainheads?
The Isiagabara[1] in particular,
Mother of all happy springs
And yet their crowned princess,
A jewel of a fountain through and through!

And what is love except
It has been fired in the kiln of trials,
And proven beyond doubt to know itself?

---

[1]Isiagbara: the name of one of the more famous springs in my hometown, Akanu Ohafia.

## XIV
## A Campaign of Beauty

Your love shall lead us through
A campaign of beauty,
And we shall overcome:
My Muse is that lady-in-arms
Whose quiver brims with verse;
Nothing can stand in her way
As nothing can stand in the way of love.
She comes! She woos! She conquers!
The woman of war who fights with beauty!
Great daughter of the peak of Olympus!
Greater even as a patroness of lovers!
And greatest for the love wars she has won!
Winner, yes, of the War of Bianca[1]!

Now watch as she wrestles
Down your father with a smile
On his face and pulls him up again
And brushes off the sand stains
On his fine body with kisses.

Does he still say no?

Love, like a vessel of twinkling stardust,
Upturned in a storm, twinkles still,
And baffles with its most tenacious light.

---

[1]The War of Bianca: an allusion to the long-drawn disagreement as the former Biafran Head of State and revered Igbo leader, Dim Chukwuemeka Odumegwu Ojukwu, also a highly skilled   poet, tried to win the approval of Chief C. C. Onoh, a prominent politician, former state governor, and businessman, to marry his lovely daughter and former beauty queen, Bianca. Incidentally, not much is said of the cardinal role of poetry in resolving the disagreement in favour of the suitor.

## XV
## The Ground beneath Your Feet

*No shaking!*[1]
The ground is firm
Beneath your feet:
Do not be afraid!

My love is here
To shield you,
To guard you,
To protect you.

Love shall live beyond
The end of time,
After death
Shall have died.

And what is fear to that
Which even death cannot subdue?

What is fear to that
Which transcends death?

What is fear to that
Which is stronger than death?

Does your father
Still say no?

---

[1]*"No shaking!"*: a Nigerian pidgin expression, popular among the urban underclass, used to reassure someone who feels threatened or afraid.

# XVI
# A Voiced Concern

Your father says he says no
Because of something
His father told him.

A voiced concern—to which
Endless generations of his offspring
Must remain bound?—A string
That might stretch thence
To the last pulse of time!

And yet he knows what Auden
Says in that immortal elegy for Yeats:
"The words of a dead man
Are modified in the guts of the living."

Could he have misunderstood his father?
Could his father's view of the future
Have been blurred for a while?
Could the prism of his soul
Have been skewed
Even for a shorter while, twisting his light
At a crucial moment
In a complicated world?

Could there have been holes
In the goatskin bag
Of his father's wisdom[1]
As there might have been
In that of my grandfather?

---

[1]Could there…/ … the goatskin…/… father's wisdom: an allusion to the remark in
Chinua Achebe's *Things Fall Apart* that wisdom is like a goatskin bag and everyone
carries his own.

What a loss to have a future
Governed by the past!

And love must scale the walls of prejudice;
For, yes, we must not know before we love,
Or build barriers of hate before we know.

"The words of a dead man
Are modified in the guts of the living."

Does your father
Still say no?

# XVII
# The Fowl of Our Birthplace

*"Ọkụkọ sị, 'Bọrọ gaa ihu; bọrọ gaa azụ;*
*nke dị n'ihu ka. "'*

Trans: "The fowl says, 'Scratch in the forward direction;
scratch backwards; that which is in front is greater.'"

— An Igbo proverb

The future must not
Hang like a tail
On the buttocks
Of the past—to be wagged
By the past
For its amusement,
Or as a wand of authority.

But it is the future's prerogative
To look to the past by choice
And not the past's place
To will the backward glance.

And, love, let us ever,
Like the fowl
Of our birthplace,
Know to scratch
For the lessons in our past
And more for the nuggets
In our future.

And may the gods
Of our birthplace
Prosper our union!

## XVIII
# Deaf and Dumb

And let me confess
That I was listless at first;
My heart was ringed with fright;
Fear still beckons,
Warning me not to love you.

But I shall dare to love you;
I dare already;
I am already daring;
I am already loving you;
I love you;
I shall always love you.

The waves of fright
May rage forever;
My ears are plugged
With the wax of your love,
And not a drop
Of their noisy tides
Can seep in.

Let it rage above my deafness!
Nor will I utter a word
Even if I have not been struck dumb
By the joy of loving you.

## XIX
## Beauty's Alchemist

My thoughts are lacquered
With the beauty of your love,
They are coated, glazed, overlaid,
Encrusted, protected like
A healthy child
In a healthy womb:
With much warmth to call its own,
Kicking, purring in silence,
Smiling with eyes closed.

None of their occasional grossness shows.

But rather they shine, reflecting
The light of your inspiration
As much as they absorb its rays.

A shining patina of gold
Flows yet again over my thoughts
From the foundry
Of your love—beauty's alchemist!

## XX
## Two Parrots

At the mention of your name
I twitch involuntarily
With excitement,
Only to learn
That it's one bird
Calling another—two birds
In love, it would seem,
Hanging head down
From a pine tree
In the harmattan,
Fighting the harsh cold
With their entwined beaks.

The one, his chest heaving,
His feathers standing
Like raised hair,
Coos a name like yours.

And how I wish it were
You and I—those parrots!

## XXI
## The Two Seducers

Always, my mind yields
To the seduction of beauty
And intelligence;
Beauty, the charmer,
Woos my mind with ease;
Intelligence, the fertilizer,
Ravishes it. And how with you
The two seducers
Had conjoined to set
My mind on heat,
Charmed by the beauty
Of your intelligence,
And yearning ever
For its soothing touch!
And now my mind's womb
Is crammed full with the joys
Of that touch—foetal poems
Kicking to break free
From its birth canal,
And like fairies
Twinkle through the earth!

## XXII
## Soul Mapping

The map of your soul
Is carved up
With boundaries of values—
An intricate work
Of divine cartography—
Invisible boundaries
Streaked with silence
And yet bold
With audible expressions.

Compassion is there, controller
Of a vast soft territory
Lush with trees
Overhung with fruits of kindness,
And faith, with a terrain of rocks
To call its own,
Hard grounds impervious
To the shafts of doubt,
And love, the queenly one
Among the best values,
The lines of whose boundaries
I now trace
With admiring fingers
To find in you
The destination of my soul.

## XXIII
# Hard Words

My words have hurt you once,
And the pain left us
Prostrate with unease,
You distraught, I nervous.

Silence dug a ditch between us;
Neither you nor I could dare cross
The wordless moat
Dark with the waters of Styx[1].

Even the ferryman of Hades[2],
His limbs and body all bone and pallor,
Would not look at me as I stood
On the dusky bank of my remorse,
Waiting to be ferried to the other side,
Ferried to meet you and be with you again,
And sprinkle watery thoughts on your heart
That burned with grief
And still glowed with warmth
Even in its distress.

O that he would relent and ferry me across
In the course of the night, my coin
Filling a chink in his palm of white bones.

O that he would take me to see
How even your sadness can be a thing of beauty,
Your face framing a charm from which words fled
Like wild birds at the sound of a gunshot,
Fled for they could not describe its forlorn loveliness.

---

[1]Styx: a river, in Greek mythology, that is the entrance to the underworld.
[2]"The ferryman of Hades": an allusion to Charon who, in Greek mythology, transported the shades of the dead across the River Styx.

My love, what a hard-tipped sword my tongue can be!
But I shall beat it into a ploughshare for your dear sake.

Nor will I ever hurt you again to rouse such charm!

## XXIV
## Your Jam Peculiar

Blue bee
Streaked with gold
And silver hues,
Come gorge yourself
With the nectar
Of my devotion;
Bright bee, bold bee, beautiful bee,
Come denude my heart
Of its pollen
Of undying love;
Then flit back
To your hive
To knead for us
The honey of high ideals
And essences, your jam
Peculiar, jellified manna,
A gift of divine labour
And grace—yours!

## XXV
# Each Time You Cry

A wish has seized
Me by the jugular,
Daring me not to grant it;
Its grip has tightened
At my throat;
Its eyes are aglare—they are emitting
Granules of ember;
Its teeth clatter
With the fury
Of its words:
"Love her! Love her! Love her!"
Says the wish,
Pressing harder at my windpipe
With each strike of its bell-like voice,
"Or fail to love her
And cease to live!"
But how come
There is laughter
In its eyes,
As there is in yours
Each time you cry?

## XXVI
## Your Sentinel Picture

A sentinel armed with beauty,
Your picture now stands
On my desktop—
On the laptop,
On the Blackberry—
The same picture
You must see
As you cross
The portal of my soul,
Frozen in a moment
Of incandescent laughter,
Your lips parted
Like the heavens
Bestowing blessings
On the earth
In a boom
Of divine grace,
Your eyes spraying twinkles
Like a fountain of stars,
Your gaiety completely pure
And out of control,
Your joy measureless
As the cosmos.

Such joy that has now engulfed me!

## XXVII
## Pilgrim and Sojourner

My soul
Once searched
For the
Holy Grail
Of good looks.

My mind
Once craved
For the
Light
Of celestial truth.

My heart
Once journeyed
To the
Paradise
Of all virtues.

My body
Once yearned
For the
Nectar
Of pure passion.

I was a pilgrim
Of many quests
And a sojourner
To many destinations.

But all that
Has ceased
For I have
Found you.

## XXVIII
## Absence

My tongue, a dreamer,
Goes to sleep
On your bosom,
Like a practiced suckling
Unwilling to outgrow
The pleasures
Of your honeyed flesh,
Your body of milk
And brown nectar
Ever flowing
And ever replenished.

How often, in your absence,
Is it lost in reveries
Of suction routines,
Working its cheeks
With pressure and release
To extract the juice
Of your sweetness
Which even absence
Cannot restrain?

## XXIX
# Song of Adoration

"The object of love is the best and most beautiful."[1]

— John Steinbeck

Your eyes are the most beautiful I have seen;
I have loved the pure charcoal blackness of their lenses
And the cheerful twinklings of their wool-white pupils,
And how their slanted lids dilate with smiles.

These I have loved at first sight and shall love
After a million million sights here and in the hereafter.
For I have wished I could see your eyes forever,
And gaze at them, and marvel in the endless
Halls crammed with the sparkling beauties they evoke.

Your hands, from elbow joints to fingertips,
Are the most beautiful I have seen;
I have loved to see their light hue glow
And have loved the feel of their palms
Which the universe of words cannot describe.

I have loved, too, how your fingernails,
The colour of marble, are trimmed down
To perfect quarter-moons—for all their marble lustre!

Your legs are beautiful too, for they make you stand tall,
And steady your gait with gentle strides, like the strides
Of whistling pines in motion, nudged by a gentle breeze.

Your body is a bell that should ring for the gods.
It is divinely beautiful in these eyes
That have never lied to me.

---

[1] From a letter by John Steinbeck to his son, Thom, published in *Steinbeck: A Life of Letters*.

## XXX
## Song of Solomon

Your body is crammed
With aphrodisiacs
Like the temple of Venus[1];
Every strand of your hair
Excites desire,
The perfume of your sweat
Is my passion's delight;
The peaches hang loose
From the tree of your bosom,
Tipped with rosy nipples.
Fruits not so forbidden!
Your straight legs
Are perfect props
For the lectern of foreplay,
Whence she, the goddess,
Preaches the sermon
Of upright love.

O that I have a million mouths!
For which, love, should I name
And not the other?
And, O, that you could strike me
With an *agaracha*[2] love, an irrevocable passion,
That I may seek to come back
However far I may run from you,
However long we're parted.

---

[1]Venus: the goddess of love in Roman mythology.
[2]*Agaracha* (Igbo); Trans: wanderer; the usage (in the expression: "*Agaracha* must come back") coveys the user's confidence that the person who has left him or her is bound to return, with a hint of the awareness of his or her indispensability to the person.

## XXXI
## White Gratitude

You have turned my life
Into a house of doves;
Each day a new bird
Hatches, whiter than the mother
That gave it birth;
That laid its egg,
Sat on it with its warm
Breast feathers,
Gave it birth.

And it is a house
Of open doors
And open windows,
Inlets never wont to close;
The birds are ever
Coming and going,
Ever leaving and returning,
All white like my gratitude.

## XXXII
## As the Leaves Grow on a Tree

I have loved to play the yogi immersed in contemplations of the divinity of your beauty, the rarity of your charms, profound and otherworldly, your ethereal looks that fuse radiant goodness and corporeal splendour.

I have loved to watch the fountain of your throat splash laughter at my face when you're happy, liquid laughter transparent as the breeze in springtime, and to see my soul levitate heavenwards with the buoyancy of your joy.

I have loved the ways you walk into my mind when you're not here, and far away, and take charge of the gilded stage of my imagination, and strut your stuff, bringing with you props of simplicity and elegance—queen of the aerial catwalks!

I have loved to love you for the sheer sake of loving you, with my mind a *tabula rasa*, a blank slate inscribed with nothing in elegant cursive, nothing but the thought of loving you ever more deeply as the days grow silently into years, as the leaves grow on a tree[1].

I have loved to envision the halo of your warmth encircle my heart in my sleep, a beatific ring of moonlight that glows with a calming touch of gentle rays, a mild luminescence that gives off a milder heat of mystery for my heart's illumination.

What more can I love about you? Many more things than I can find words for! Many more of which only silence can dare to speak with the awe of gratitude! Many more! My darling, my love!

---

[1]As… tree: John Keats uses the same expression in his famous letter to John Taylor that reflects on the characteristics of poetry, including how it should originate.

## XXXIII
# Endearments

Goddess of enchantment,
I await the boon of your return;

Cyclic meteor and seasonal moon,
I await the boon of your return;

Gold light and silver penumbra,
I await the boon of your return;

Eclipser of darkness with rosy rays,
I await the boon of your return;

Radicle of my deep faith,
I await the boon of your return;

Plumule of my high ideals,
I await the boon of your return;

White tide of my resonant joys,
I await the boon of your return;

Nectar of my heart's devotion,
O, I await the boon of your return!

## XXXIV
# When I Meet You

Will the cock crow
When I meet you,
The cock that crows
A new dawn into being?

Will the meteor hurtle
Through the sky,
A star dying
So many more
Can be born,
An epochal sign
Of the coming of new
And better and greater things?

Will the earth shake
To its rocky bed?
Will the sun stand still
For a while
Or the moon pause
In its orbit?

What will happen
When I meet you?
I wonder!

## XXXV
## Down to Home

It was almost dusk
When you arrived,
Trailing a new radiance,
A half-crepuscular light
Arched above the rainbow.

Charm, gaiety, poise,
And that simple grandeur
With which the foundations
Of beauty were laid—they all
Came with you—a willing retinue,
A sober cavalcade
With the mild effervescence
Of your descent
From the upper blues.

And we sat at a table,
Just the two of us,
And I watched, delighted, under a calm light,
As you cracked eggs of wit
With your soft knuckles,
And shelled them, and held them
In your fingers like delicate forceps,
And passed them to your mouth
Gated with glistening white teeth.
A rare beauty that feeds on wit!

And I saw the sudden film of tears
Spread over your eyes
When I spoke of a distressed child!
So compassion, too, came with you—
The last, perhaps, of that retinue, that cavalcade.
Or weren't there others I could not see?

Yet, seen or not, I would love
To be with you, whose heart's potion
Flows down to home, a tonic
And a salve for places of distress,
If my heart can get that
Which it desires.

## XXXVI
## Woman of the East

Woman of the East,
Womb and cradle of light,
I see you and a feeling strikes me
As if the sun is rising from my heart,
As if my heart will burst open
With a million golden rays,
A gazillion spindles of sharp, luminous joy.

Your smile is like a rose
Unfolding its blossom
To greet the dawn;
You laughter is like a heavenly cackle
Emitting showers
Of granular light,
As when a firecracker
Pours down its twinkling motes
Like spores from midair.

Your hips are a curvaceous wonder,
A fleshy marvel of shapeliness
And rhythm
In fluid motion;
Your stride is like the walk
Of the lioness,
Leisurely and self-assured;
And when you speak,
I recall the breeze
Rocking the April cradle
Of new leaves and flowers,
Woman of the East!

## XXXVII
# The Pledge

I love you more than tongue can tell,
With a love that'll keep you glad and well,
That'll shield you from the storms of life,
And make you, most of all, my wife.

Yes, when the storms of life shall break,
Through every tremor, every quake,
When the grounds you know may crack and shake,
I'll be a protector for your sake.

In the midst of light I'll be your love,
And when it's dark I'll love you more;
Past every shadow, every hue,
My love for you shall shine as true.

O, down the valley, up the hill,
I'll love you ever, love you still;
With my head and heart in full accord,
All these I pledge, so help me God!

## XXXVIII
## I Give Thanks

Loving you has raised
Me in the estimation
Of my Muse, and I shall
Give thanks though my heart
Aches from breaking slowly.

The joys of love
Are not measured
By their length
But by the strength or beauty
Of what lights they shed
In their blazing journeys
Through our hearts,
Their winged flights
Of doubt and ecstasy.

Loving you has shed
Its many-coloured light,
Has lit my heart
With the spectrum
Of its brilliance.

And that light has shed
Its lessons to swell
The secrets in my soul.

And ever shall I hold
Those secrets dear
For your sake.

## XXXIX
## Rocks on Our Path

A mortal seeking perfection
From a mortal in a world
Whose "divinities" are flawed.

Words that now stream
With inconsistency.

The disguised traps
Of an alien and fluid faith
Which neither you nor I
May fully fathom.

These are the rocks that now rise
On our path to a blissful union,
Boulders I could blow away
With the breath of reason!

O that you may not surmount them
Even now your father has said yes!
O that you may not surmount them!

## XL
## Your Voice Still Flows

With a buzz of mellifluous ease,
Your voice still flows
Like the zephyr
Over the savannah:
No taller grass
Disrupts its gentle course.

Today I have heard it
As never before: smooth,
Soft, measured, pulsating
With ripples of serenity.

And I have wondered
That it could be so calm
Amid the turmoil
Now raging in my soul.

## XLI
# Because I Loved You

Your love is the perch
From which
My verse shall spring
And spread its wings
And soar heavenwards
To immortality, buoyed by
The benign winds
Of the gracious Muses.

The world shall read of you
And love you because
I loved you,
And your name shall
Taste like nectar on the tongue
Of every soul that walks the earth
And shall be etched
Even on stony hearts
And engraved on watery minds,
A memory beyond time and place,
Defiant of the worms of the grave
And of the gritty teeth of decay
That gnaw down all
But the sublime and imperishable.

## XLII
## The Harmattan

Our people say: "If you fail
To lick your lips in the harmattan
The harmattan will lick them for you."
And how I must mind
The season when the savannah
Turns a colour as if scorched
But not by fire, and the moistureless wind,
Shaking down the dead leaves,
Rustles over the grass
And hoists the feathers
Of the moulting hen
On its swirling eddies.

And how I must mind the season
As that in which I must be mindful
To moisten the lips of your heart's
Deepest needs with a surplus of love!

## XLIII
## The Potter

You would love to change me,
I know, to create beauty
Out of my grossness,
To mould me into the most beautiful clay pot
That ever passed through your potter's hands.

That is good, my love,
A wish that stirs my heart with gratitude.

But don't our people say:
"To mould a clay pot, one
Must first gather the clay.[1]"?

And you have yet to gather me,
To dredge me out of the riverbank
Of your doubts and make me yours.

I only have gathered you,
Have claimed you with an unwavering faith
In the goodness of your heart
And the brightness of our future together.

You have yet to gather me,
You have yet to accept me,
So I slip like ghost clay through your potter's hands!

---

[1]"To mould a clay pot, one/Must first gather the clay": "*O bu onye kotachaa uro tupu o kpuba ite.*"—An Igbo proverb.

## XLIV
## Light Has Departed

In my heart light has departed,
And the vacuum is filled with gloom:
My blood gropes about the chamber
Wondering where to go
As darkness drops a veil
Across its wonted course.

My aorta is stoppered, and
The darkness of your indecision
Is the cork that bars blood
From its inflamed gut.

Soon our souls shall stand on
The tightrope of the Equator,
Mine facing East, yours West,
That each step they take may
Bring them farther apart,
And a backward glance
Incline mine to lose its balance
And drop into the abyss, done
With your memories forever.

Alas, two souls to be divorced
Before they would marry!
Alas, two souls to be prised asunder
Before their nuptials!
One perhaps happy, the other
Lost in a maze of misery;
One perhaps cheerful
Like the russet dawn in spring,
The other cheerless
Like a harmattan dusk.

Alas: they may ever walk the Equator
As though on a tightrope,
Facing East and West,
Seeking till the end of time
To keep their balance.

## XLV
# A Necklace of Grief

Love, treasure slipping through my grasping hands,
I had written you on scrolls of gold,
Now I write you on parchments of lead
From a heart whose pains
Are achingly alive!

A necklace of grief hangs on my neck;
It is golden with a silver pendant,
And heavier than lead.

I did not choose to wear it;
But your unsure ways have hung it on my neck,
Not my neck but the neck of my heart.

Nor do I even know whether to call it my neck
Or the neck of my heart where the necklace
Hangs with its golden chain and silver pendant
And a dull heaviness worse than lead.

Yes, it is a legacy of your unsure ways,
My inheritance from your doubts,
My albatross from your indecisions,
A sombre piece of jewellery that I must
Wear with gloom and reluctance
And only wish I knew for how long.

## XLVI
# The Metamorphosis

Yesterday, only yesterday,
Your love became to me
Like the echo of raindrops
Fading in the distant rooftops,
A dream that merged
With twilight
Before it dawned,
A seed snapped up
By a hungry bird
On the verge of its sprouting,
A spring to be held back
Forever in the bowels
Of a grim rock.

It became, too, like the whiff
Of Ethiopian coffee
To be drunk only by inhalation,
A vapour laden with pleasure,
Light and tantalising,
Teasing the taste buds
With its deep dark brew,
Its sweet unattainability,
And laughing while
It teased them
To their death.

And how such cruelty
Had seemed foreign
To its nature
In the beginning!

## XLVII
## Fear

Always love, like progress,
Like creation,
Is a fruit that grows
On the tree of faith and courage,
And error goes to fertilise its being,
Feeding nutrients to
Its hungry roots,
Nutrients of knowledge
That stems in part
From error.

For fearing to err
We may make nothing
And surely cannot create love.

Fear, the enemy of progress,
Of creation,
Has ringed your eyes
With a cold fire,
And dug a moat of ice
Right round your heart,
Fear that is also
The bane of love,
Fear!

## XLVIII
## The No Your Father Said

Every falsehood has a lifespan.

Now I know that the no
Your father said
Was the no you wanted to say
Through your father's voice,
Your ventriloquial no!
For now your father
Has said yes
Your feet are both stiff
And frozen
As if
The spirit of death
Has flowed
Through them.

And your tongue
Is cleaved
To your palate
In a strange marriage
Of guile and silence.

Nor shall it sway me
If you were to ever
Speak again!

And lest you forget:
Ripe fruits that keep late
On the boughs
Risk being eaten by bats.

## XLIX
## That We Could Disprove Hemingway

Would that we could disprove Hemingway
When he says, "If two people love each other,
there can be no happy end to it.[1]"

Would that we could prove false
His bitter truth,
And show by our mutual lot
That the end of love
Can be happy.

Would, o would, that we could disprove Hemingway
When he says, "If two people love each other,
there can be no happy end to it."

But alas we too have not disproved his words!
Nor have any two who ever loved?

Ever soft and tender are the sweet beginnings of love,
And ever hard and sore its bitter end.

---

[1]From *Death in the Afternoon.*

# L
## Lament

Soaked, drenched, bedraggled,
Worse than a fowl
Sodden to the quills,
I shiver at the thought
Of this falling night,
This night
Of our affection
Falling cumbrously
Like a weight of dull feathers,
This night in which my hopes
Plummet to the dust
In the wings of waiting.

This night in which my heart
Must not be heard,
As it licks the bitter sweets of love!

This night in which my heart
Must not be heard,
As it chews the bitter cud of love!

Would that the ground
Could yawn and suck
Me into its bowels
And clap its lips shut forever!

But time, ready with solace
And breasts gorged
For my orphaned heart,
Stands firm beside me
And speaks, softly:
"Tone down your grief, love's poet:
Love's dawn
Shall ever break
For those who love."

## LI
# The Brief Candle

The candle of my joy in your love
Has burnt ever so briefly.
The flame has sputtered
To its death
Never to resurrect
Or be lit again.
The strong fist
Of the west wind
Has knocked it down
From its gilt mantelpiece
Where it shall never stand again.
It lies on the cold floor, extinguished,
Snuffed out with its head-ward fall,
Its short wick trailing a white smoke.
This candle shall burn no more, nevermore!

And I, like a heifer vanquished
In a fight for a mate,
Must slink away in retreat,
Crestfallen, on a sad journey
Whence I have always returned
And shall again return.

For a man born to love
Will yield not to one
Or a thousand defeats
At love's battlefield,
And vanquished and flattened a million times
He will dare to rise again and love afresh,
Doubling yet his vigour with each fall.

Of love's sweet and bitter ways I shall never tire,
My zeal for loving shall never expire,
And ever shall I nurse a deep desire
To light keen hearts with love's eternal fire.

## LII
## Envoi

"...the body of love will still
be breathing upon earth!...[1]"

— Pablo Neruda

Once beaten, twice stronger:
I shall sing of love again,
And forever yield my heart and soul
To the endless march of affection.

My roots shall find
Their natural soil
In another's heart
And shall grow relentlessly
Downward to the bedrock
Of her soul, drawing moisture and nutriment,
And the tree of our love
Shall grow to an oaken stoutness,
Spreading its arms, fruit-laden, towards the heavens,
Standing up forever to the elements,
To rain, heat, fire and floods,
And to snow, storms, lightning and thunder,
Shedding fresh breath at night,
Gleaming forever in the sun.

Mine is still the Midas touch for love,
And all I touch anon will turn to love!

---

[1]From "Ode and Burgeoning," in the New Directions edition of *The Captain's Verses*, translated by Donald D. Walsh.

# Appendix

## Music Scores

"Music is the purest form of art ...
therefore true poets, they who are
seers, seek to express the universe
in terms of music."

— Rabindranath Tagore

# I

# Maple Country
### (The Canada Day Song)

*Words and Melody by* **Ikeogu Oke**
*Arranged by* **Jude Nwankwo**

**Andante Moderato**

Verse 1

Land of the leaf like the o - pen hand, Vast, free-giv-ing and

Piano

warm. Land of the red___ ma - ple leaf, We sa - lute

Pno.

you! All hail! Beau-ti - ful land! Glo-rious in - deed___ and

**Chorus**

Pno.

Maple Country

Free - giv - er of grace and good health; O, land of peace__ and gen - tle strength, We sa - lute you!

*D.S. al Fine*  **Verse 4**

It is your day__ and we__ are here, Friends of the earth and friends for you, To ho-nour you__ and share__ your joy, Ma - ple coun - - try!

*D.S. al Fine*

# II

# A Gandhian Prayer

*Words and Melody by* **Ikeogu Oke**

*Arranged by* **Jude Nwankwo**

Dear Lord, ne-ver cease to grant your fa - vours To those who prey on wri - ters _____ and their la - bours; May their barns be ev-er filled with mon-ey, May their days be ev-er bright and

sun - ny. May their child-ren ne - ver cease to pros - per In

health and rich-es, as is fair and pro-per, And may their wives be hap-pier than they

wish,___ And ne-ver let their bles-sings di - mi - nish. And

if they think it's hu-man___ to be mean,___ That it's their hap-less vic-tims___ they de-

mean,_____ Dear Lord, raise their poor souls from the gut - ter In

which, like drunk-en elves, they crawl or tot-ter. Then cure their blind-ness_____that their eyes may

see_____ That there's no vir-tue in dis-ho-nes - ty.

# III

# I Can't Reach You

Words and Melody by **Ikeogu Oke**
Arranged by **Jude Nwankwo**

oth - er,___ More tru-ly than a moth-er.___ Ba-by, ba-by, I'm wait - ing, Ba-by, ba-by,

I'm wait - ing, I want to be your man. Please call me once you can. Ba-by, ba-by,

I'm wait - ing. Ba-by, ba-by. I'm wait - ing, To love you like no oth-er,___ More tru-ly than a

moth - er.___ I'm wait - ing by the___

I'm wait - ing, Ba-by, ba-by. I'm wait - in, To love you like no oth-er.____ More tru-ly than a

moth - er.____

# IV

# The Pledge

Words and Melody by **Ikeogu Oke**
Arranged by **Jude Nwankwo**